Kingdom Files:

Who Was Esther?

Kingdom Files:

Who Was Esther?

Matt Koceich

BARBOUR BOOKS

An Imprint of Barbour Publishing, Inc.

Print ISBN 978-1-68322-629-1

eBook Editions:
Adobe Digital Edition (.epub) 978-1-68322-897-4
Kindle and MobiPocket Edition (.prc) 978-1-68322-903-2

Cover design by C. B. Canga
Interior illustration by Patricia Yuste

Published by Barbour Books, an imprint of Barbour Publishing, Inc., 1810 Barbour Drive, Uhrichsville, Ohio 44683, www.barbourbooks.com

Our mission is to inspire the world with the life-changing message of the Bible.

Member of the
Evangelical Christian
Publishers Association

Printed in the United States of America.

06136 0718 CM

Dear Reading Detective,

Welcome to Kingdom Files! You're now a very important part of the Kingdom Files investigation—a series of really cool biographies all found in the Bible. Each case you investigate focuses on an important Bible character and is separated into three sections to make your time fun and interesting. First, you'll find the **Fact File**, which contains key information about a specific Bible character whom God called to do big things for His kingdom. Next, you'll read through an **Action File** that lays out Bible events showing the character in action. And finally, the **Power File** is where you'll find valuable information and memory verses to help you see how God is working in your life too. Along the way, **Clue Boxes** will offer applications to help you keep track of your thoughts as you make your way through the files. You can also use these sections to record questions you might have along Esther's journey. Write down any questions, and then ask your parents to get them involved in your quest.

Before you begin, know this: not only did God have plans for the Bible characters you'll read about in the Kingdom Files, but Jeremiah 29:11 says that God has big plans for you too! I pray that *Kingdom Files: Who Was Esther?* helps you get a bigger picture of God, and that you will see just how much He loves you!

Blessings,

M.K.

Name: **Esther**

Occupation: **queen of Persia**

From: **Persia**

Years Active: **483–473 BC**

Kingdom Work: **served as a queen and helped save the lives of many people**

Key Stats:
+ The Jewish people are threatened by an evil plot.

+ Esther has the courage to stand up for her people.

+ The Jews are saved from destruction!

Mini Timeline:

538 BC
First exiles
return to
Jerusalem

486 BC
Xerxes
becomes
king of
Persia

479 BC
Esther
becomes
queen

1

A King, a Party, and a Queen

The book of Esther gives us hope that God cares all about our daily lives. Whether it's something personal that we struggle with like being anxious, or problems with other people like being bullied or feeling left out, studying Esther's story will encourage us to remember that God is in control and always on our side. It's a story of hope that reminds us that God is our Protector and He cares about all the things that we care about.

Our investigation into the life of Esther begins in a land called Persia in the year 483 BC. Persia was a place in the Middle East. If you find Iran on a world map, you will see where Persia was located. Persia covered so much land back in the time of Esther that it was known as an empire. To get an idea of how large Persia was, look back at the world map and find Greece. Now look right until you find India. All the land in between was Persia!

Esther's story starts with a king, a party, and a queen. Esther's parents were most likely a part of the people from Jerusalem who were exiled to Babylon under the rule of King Nebuchadnezzar. *Exiled* means people are forced to move far away from their homes. As was the case for Esther's parents, they were made to move to a foreign country that had a different culture and different language.

The book of Esther takes place 103 years after the Jewish people were taken captive, and 54 years after a man named Zerubbabel led the first group of exiles back from Persia to their homeland in Jerusalem.

The Persian king, Cyrus, said that the captives could return to Jerusalem; however, many of the Jewish people decided to stay in Persia. Esther's parents were part of the group that did not want to return to their homeland.

CLUES

Even though He is not mentioned by name, God is not absent from the book of Esther. He is there from the very first chapter as we read about the setting into which Esther will eventually arrive. We see how God goes before Esther to set up the perfect situation for her to enter into the king's castle—not as a bystander, but as the queen!

Esther's story takes place in a nation called Persia and Media. This was the most powerful nation in the world at the time. A proud king named Xerxes was in charge of this massive kingdom that stretched all the way from Ethiopia to

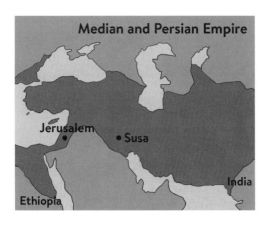

Median and Persian Empire

India—127 provinces in all. While there were palaces all over the land, a very large one was located at a place called Susa. Xerxes wanted to throw a big party for all his officials and leaders so he could show off everything that he had accomplished.

Xerxes was very rich and liked to have fun, so he decided to make the party last for 180 days! This six-month

CLUES

Xerxes was most likely trying to show off in front of military leaders so they would want to join his army.

festival would show off how glorious his kingdom
was. The Bible tells us that after that huge party
was over, the king hosted another party that
lasted for seven days. This second party was for
all the people who lived in the city. No matter if
they were rich or poor, the king invited them in,
and they all were served in the gardens. This was
a beautiful display of the king's money and power.
The people sat on couches made of gold and silver

and drank from golden cups. White and blue linens hung from marble pillars all around the garden. The king made sure everyone received the royal treatment!

The queen at that time was Vashti, and she liked to throw parties too. The Bible says that while all the king's festivities were happening, Vashti was hosting a banquet for the women in the palace. It was customary for women not to appear in public, so the queen had her own gathering for the ladies.

The king sent his men to bring his queen to the

party so he could show everyone how beautiful she was. But the queen refused to go! No one knows why she refused, but this was where all the weeks of fun came to an abrupt end. Vashti did not do as the king ordered, so "the king became furious and burned with anger" (1:12). And even though Esther hasn't been mentioned in the story yet, this scene sets up the reason she was called out of her everyday life and into God's kingdom work!

Xerxes summoned all the people who were closest to him, his advisers, and asked what he should do. They all said he should punish Vashti because if she wouldn't obey the king, then all the other noblewomen in the kingdom might act in the same way. That sounds silly, but way back then, things were different. The biggest responsibility the advisers had was to make sure no one disrespected the king! King Xerxes needed

to act quickly, and that's exactly what he did.

The first royal decree was sent out: Vashti
was not allowed in the king's presence. She was
no longer the queen. Her behavior didn't please
the king, so a new queen would need to be found.
And just like that, Vashti was out. The king made
another order. A second decree went out: "Every
man should be ruler over his own household"
(1:22). At that time, a royal decree could not be
undone. Vashti could never be queen again.

God was using this very unfortunate situation to make a way for Esther to enter into the king's palace.

A New Queen

Four long years passed between Vashti's removal as queen and Esther's arrival. The king and his army had battled against Greece. Back in Bible times, there were a lot of battles fought to gain or keep control of land. The Persian Empire covered so much land that Xerxes, as king, had to fight many battles to keep his rule strong. He was not successful, and so the king was back in the palace, defeated and all alone. King Xerxes thought about Vashti, but because of the royal order he had given, she could not come back.

CLUES

God was not far away. He was using Vashti's dismissal as a way to eventually protect His people.

The king's servants came to Xerxes and told him to order a search for a new queen. Xerxes liked this idea, so word was sent throughout the kingdom. This is where Esther came into the picture. She had an older cousin named Mordecai. Mordecai was a man who lived in the Persian city of Susa. He most likely worked for the king because of his position at the city gate. Seeing that

Esther had been orphaned, Mordecai adopted and raised Esther "as his own daughter when her mother and father died" (2:7). At some time during the search for a new queen, Esther was brought to the palace.

Esther was part of a group of young women taken from their everyday lives and brought to the king's castle. One day she was doing her normal routine—drawing water from a well, playing games, and buying vegetables at the local market—and the next she was being whisked away by the king's soldiers. Esther must have been anxious and unsure about her future, but she trusted God. This was also hard for Esther, because she was taken from her only relative. Away from Mordecai, the only family she had left, Esther was escorted to the castle and forced to grow up in a hurry. She was surely confused about her new position, but Esther never stopped believing that God was in charge of her life.

At the palace, Esther immediately found favor with a man named Hegai, who was in charge of finding the next queen. Esther even received "beauty treatments and special food" (2:9). While all this was happening, Esther did not tell anyone that she was Jewish. Mordecai had instructed her not to say anything about her background. He had a feeling that things wouldn't go well if the king and his assembly knew Esther was Jewish.

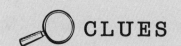 **CLUES**

Esther's Hebrew name was Hadassah, which means "myrtle," but her Persian name was Esther.

Esther respected her cousin's wishes and kept her identity a secret.

While all this beauty work was going on, Mordecai stuck close to the palace courtyard where Esther was so he would know how she was doing. He wanted to make sure no harm came her way. Mordecai showed that he was a loyal man by caring for Esther.

For one whole year, Esther and the other women went through a process of beauty treatments to look nice: "six months with oil of myrrh and six with perfumes and cosmetics" (2:12). The Bible says that Esther won the favor of everyone who saw her, even the king.

On the surface, Esther's story is very similar to our spiritual life stories

because she was taken from a faraway place into the presence of a king, just as Jesus saves us from our sins and brings us into His Father's house!

3

A Conspiracy and a Very Bad Plan

After many days of training and preparing, the time
had come for Esther to go to the king. Standing in
the royal palace, she soon learned that the king liked
her more than any of the other young ladies he had
seen. Xerxes took the royal crown and placed it on
Esther's head. This act made her the queen of the
whole land of
Persia!

Awhile
later, Mordecai
was again
at the king's
gate keeping
watch and
overheard two

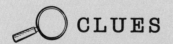

CLUES

You can see God orchestrating events so that Esther will be seen in an even bigger and better light.

of the king's officials, Bigthana and Teresh, talking about an evil plan. The men were scheming to take Xerxes' life. Mordecai knew what had to be done. He told Queen Esther, "who in turn reported it to the king, giving credit to Mordecai" (2:22). Because of Mordecai's quick thinking, the king was safe.

Things were going well for Xerxes. He had a new queen, and his empire was still the largest in the land. Sometime later the king promoted a man named Haman to a seat of special honor that put him in a very high position over all the other nobles. The king called for all the royal officials to kneel before Haman at the city gate. Remember, Mordecai held a position in the king's court, but

he refused to obey the rule and would not bow to
Haman. This was because Mordecai obeyed God.
He had the courage not to give in to the king's
order.

The royal officials saw that Mordecai refused
to bow to Haman and questioned him about it.
"Day after day they spoke to him but he refused
to comply" (3:4). The men took the report back to

Haman, who became furious when he saw that Mordecai would not honor him. Haman was in a position of authority. When he heard that Mordecai was a Jew, he wanted to find a way to destroy not only Mordecai but all the Jewish people "throughout the whole kingdom of Xerxes" (3:6).

Haman found himself in the company of the king and told him all about Mordecai's disrespect and the others who did not do as they were told. "Their customs are different from those of all other people, and they do not obey the king's laws; it is not in the king's best interest to tolerate them" (3:8). This was exactly what Mordecai was trying to warn Esther about. Esther was about to face a very big problem that would require great courage on her part. Haman wanted to do away with the Jewish people, and Mordecai knew that the king would more than likely sign a decree to help Haman accomplish his evil plan.

Xerxes agreed with Haman and even told him he could attack the Jewish people. The king took off his signet ring and gave it to Haman. Orders would be written up so that Jewish people in every province across the kingdom would be under attack. The king's ring would be used to seal the orders so the people would know the orders were officially from the king. Xerxes gave his chief official full authority to do great harm to Esther's people. All because Mordecai refused to kneel before Haman.

Remember...Queen Esther was Jewish too!

The plan that Haman tried to carry out was very evil. Haman wanted to take the lives of all the Jews who lived all throughout the king's realm. His plan was publicized everywhere. This terrible moment was one that God wouldn't stand for. Even though the situation looked bleak, God was at work behind the scenes.

Mordecai Asks Esther to Help

When Mordecai heard of Haman's plan, he was very sad. "He tore his clothes, put on sackcloth and ashes, and went out into the city, wailing loudly and bitterly" (4:1). The situation seemed hopeless, and Mordecai couldn't contain his emotions. He must have felt responsible for the threat that was now against the Jews. Things just kept getting worse, and Mordecai couldn't see

how the situation would ever change.

People couldn't help but wonder about the grown man who was tearing his clothes in the middle of the street and wailing. They stopped and stared at the man covered in ashes and sackcloth. Some of them knew that Mordecai and Esther were related, and they sent word about Mordecai's actions back to Esther. She had clothes sent to him, but he refused to put them on. Wearing sackcloth was a sign of seeking forgiveness and humbling oneself before God. And Mordecai knew the only way out of this situation would be through the power of God.

Esther sent one of her helpers to find Mordecai to see what was bothering him. Hathak went out and listened as Mordecai retold all the terrible things that Haman planned to do to the Jewish people. Mordecai asked Hathak to have

Esther go to the king and "beg for mercy and plead with him for her people" (4:8).

Esther was concerned because Mordecai's request would put her in a very dangerous position. Anyone who approached the king uninvited, including the queen, would be severely punished. She told Hathak to go back to Mordecai and tell him that anyone who went to the king without being summoned would be put to death, unless the king extended the gold scepter to them and spared their life.

Mordecai had a sobering reply for the queen: "Do not think that because you are in the king's house you alone of all the Jews will escape" (4:13). Mordecai wasn't about to give up trying to get Esther to see how serious the situation was. He went on to tell her that if she didn't do anything to help, the Jewish people would receive deliverance from another place. This means that

God would protect His people. If Esther didn't act to help the situation, God would still keep His word because He is a promise keeper.

Esther knew that the time had come to make a choice. She didn't waste a moment. The queen instructed Mordecai to gather all the Jews who lived in the region and have them fast—not eat or drink anything—for three days. Esther added that she too would do the same

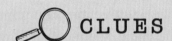 **CLUES**

Mordecai knew it was time for Esther to put her complete trust in God. It wasn't going to be easy, but it was what she had to do.

thing. She promised Mordecai that after her fasting period was done, she would go to the king, "even though it is against the law. And if I perish, I perish" (4:16). Esther was willing to risk her own life for the sake of all her people. She was willing to put others above herself.

Esther is a great example of submitting to God even in very difficult times.

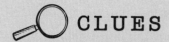 CLUES

Fasting is a common practice all throughout the Bible. Jesus even fasted for a very long time to be able to focus on God's will for His life. Fasting helped a person rely on God instead of relying on things of the world.

Esther's Plan

Esther had the courage to be a woman of her word. Remember, she was queen! In terms of money and comfort, Esther was all set. She didn't need anything. But in her heart, she knew that Mordecai was right. God had brought her to this position of influence for a very important reason. Her people were depending on her. After fasting for three whole days, Esther mustered up the faith it took to stand before the king, knowing that God was on her side.

Esther was ready to go to Xerxes and confront him about Haman's terrible idea. But first she needed to gain the king's trust before she would reveal the evil plot. She went to the king's hall and waited to speak to Xerxes.

He asked what she needed and said, "Even up to half the kingdom, it will be given you" (5:3). Esther's plan included inviting the king and Haman to a banquet that she personally prepared. She wanted them to let their guards down and be happy. The king quickly accepted her invitation. "Bring Haman at once. . .so that we may do what Esther asks" (5:5).

At the banquet, the king and Haman

CLUES

Esther is a great role model because she didn't let fear stop her from doing the right thing. She trusted that God was big enough to handle her problems. Knowing that truth, she stepped out in faith and acted.

were present, enjoying the meal that Esther had prepared for them. Xerxes, again, asked Esther what she wanted: "Now what is your petition? It will be given you. And what is your request? Even up to half the kingdom, it will be granted"

(5:6). Esther thought about it, but she knew the time wasn't right to discuss the situation with the king. She wasn't going to back down, but she was going to wait on God's timing. Another invitation had to come first. Esther replied to the king with another offer. She invited the king to bring Haman to a second banquet the following day. She would prepare another extraordinary dining experience. After she invited them, Esther said, "Then I will answer the king's question" (5:8).

Twice Esther waited to give her specific request that the king protect her people. The whole time they enjoyed the wide variety of food and drink, Esther was preparing to take her request to the king. Don't forget she had fasted to make sure things were right between her and God. Waiting on God's perfect timing was something Esther was trying hard to do.

Meanwhile, Haman was out walking and was "happy and in high spirits" (5:9). He thought it was wonderful to be treated with such respect. He felt proud to be honored with all of these fancy meals. What a feast he enjoyed at the favor of Queen Esther! If she put together such an awesome meal for him, all the officials he would come in contact with should surely bow to him and treat him with the same respect. That's when he came across Mordecai at the king's gate.

This time Haman was determined that

Mordecai would bow. However, yet again, Mordecai didn't bow or show fear toward Haman. This greatly angered the king's official. The Bible says that Haman was filled with rage—intense anger—against Mordecai but restrained himself and went home (5:9–10). Haman was really mad at Mordecai, but he controlled his feelings and didn't say anything to him.

Haman was rather selfish, and when he arrived home, he called his friends and wife, Zeresh, and began boasting to them about his wealth and his many children. This was a man who liked the way things looked on the outside but didn't care about what was on the inside.

Mordecai had irritated him by not bowing to him. To Haman, that was very disrespectful. Haman bragged to his wife and friends so he could feel good about himself.

He was also very happy to announce that the king had "elevated him above the other nobles and officials" (5:11). This was a very proud moment for the king's highest official. He had been invited to a private banquet with the king and queen and elevated to a high-ranking position in the king's court. This was his time to shine. Haman believed that all of these titles and connections made him more important than he really was.

Haman was not at a loss for finding ways to praise himself. He went on to tell his friends that he was the only person Queen Esther invited along with the king to the banquet. But then Haman admitted that even with all those gifts, he was still angry and depressed because he kept seeing Mordecai at the king's gate. He told his family and friends that the man always refused to bow down to him. This was unacceptable to Haman, and he wanted something to be done to teach Mordecai a lesson.

After she listened to her husband's complaints, Haman's wife had an answer. She gave her husband an idea to set up a pole that was roughly seventy-five feet tall. This would become a thing called a gallows. The gallows were used in Bible times as a punishment to hang someone who had committed a crime. The gallows had two poles connected by a cross bar. From the cross bar, there would hang a rope. Haman's wife said that she wanted Mordecai to die on the gallows. Zeresh told her husband to go to the king and share their idea. She figured that if this man Mordecai was such a problem for her husband, then he should be done away with. Haman listened to his wife and had the pole set up. Then he went to the banquet with King Xerxes, excited to share his wife's idea.

What Happened Next

The Bible says that the king couldn't sleep, so he had his people bring the book of chronicles to him and read it out loud. The chronicles were

books of history. As he listened to all the accomplishments of his people and his empire, Xerxes learned about how Mordecai uncovered the officials' plot to take the life of the king. Xerxes couldn't believe it. He asked what special honor had been given to Mordecai for his bravery in saving the king's life. "Nothing has been done for him," was the answer (6:3).

The king asked who was there in the court to help honor Mordecai. Now, while all this was going on, Haman entered the court to tell the king about his new evil plan to kill Mordecai. Xerxes ordered Haman to be brought in. From Haman's view, it was good news that the king was going to hear about his plan to do away with Mordecai.

The king asked Haman what should be done for a person he wanted to honor. Haman thought Xerxes was talking about him, so he said the person deserved to wear one of the king's royal robes and ride on one of the king's horses through the city. Haman's selfish pride was growing. He couldn't be happier. His king was about to reward him in a big way!

The king liked what Haman had suggested and ordered him to go and get the things he mentioned. Haman obeyed. Can you picture the pride growing inside Haman? Can you picture the smile on his face as he went to get the piece of clothing that would make him look like royalty? Haman collected the royal robe and one of the king's horses and brought them both back to the king. It was almost time to wear the robe and ride around on the king's horse, having everyone give him praise.

King Xerxes then told Haman news that he never would have imagined the king would tell him. Haman's mouth must have dropped open when Xerxes said that all of those things were for Mordecai. The Bible says Haman "robed Mordecai, and led him on horseback through the city streets" (6:11).

After the humiliating experience of having to

shower praise on Mordecai, Haman raced home and told his wife the bad news. His wife and friends warned him that it wouldn't be a good idea to stand in Mordecai's way. Haman was confused. But there was still the banquet. . . Things weren't all that bad.

The king's men soon came to take Haman to the banquet Esther had invited him to. He had been humiliated, and now it was time to go back

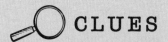

CLUES

Can you imagine? First, Haman was trying to harm Mordecai, but now he was being made to parade the man around to gain honor from the people. Haman had to watch his enemy get the praise that he wanted for himself. Surely Mordecai couldn't believe it either!

to the king. Haman's life was a mess, and he hoped that something would change for the better—and soon.

Haman's Fate

At the banquet, the king again asked Esther what it was that she wanted. The time had come for Esther to stick up for what was right. She told Xerxes that what she wanted more than anything was for her people to be spared. This is when she made the big announcement. Esther was about to speak the one thing that Mordecai told her not to speak. Queen Xerxes told the king that she too was Jewish. "For I and my people have been sold to be destroyed" (7:4).

Right there at table, the king asked Esther who the person was behind all these accusations, and she said, "An adversary and enemy! This vile Haman!" (7:6).

Right then Haman was very afraid. Not only

was he not receiving the praise he desired, but now Esther had told the king about his plan.

King Xerxes was so mad that he got up from the table and went outside to the palace gardens. Haman knew that his life was in danger, so he stayed with Esther, asking her to spare his life. The Bible says that he sat on her couch begging her. Meanwhile, the king came back in from the gardens and saw Haman talking with Esther.

Xerxes thought Haman was trying to hurt his

queen. To make matters worse, one of the king's helpers took the opportunity to tell Xerxes about the gallows that Haman had built to kill Mordecai. The king was furious and ordered Haman's life to be taken on the same pole instead. Afterward, the Bible says that "the king's fury subsided" (7:10).

On the same day, the king gave Queen Esther all of Haman's estate. Xerxes also invited Mordecai to come into his presence because Esther had told the king how they were related. Then the king gave Mordecai his signet ring, and Esther appointed Mordecai to be in charge of Haman's estate. What a turn of events! Everything that Haman had wanted was given to Mordecai.

Esther again pleaded with Xerxes so that he would stop the evil plan Haman had created to destroy the Jewish people. "Let an order be written overruling the dispatches that Haman... devised and wrote to destroy the Jews in all the king's provinces" (8:5). The king gave Mordecai permission to write a letter that gave the Jews permission to arm themselves and defend their families. This meant that they were now protected under order of the king. The order was posted in public places "so that the Jews would be ready on that day to avenge themselves on their enemies" (8:13).

Esther's boldness resulted in salvation for her

people. She refused to let evil intimidate her. Her courage to approach the king with the request for Xerxes to protect her people resulted in the saving of many lives. "For the Jews, it was a time of happiness and joy, gladness and honor" (8:16).

Because of God's faithfulness and Esther's desire to serve her Creator, all the Jewish people were defended and saved.

In the End

God used Mordecai to help take care of and protect Esther, just like He used Esther to help take care of and protect the Jewish people. The Bible says that Mordecai became more powerful and well-known throughout the kingdom. His reputation spread across the land, and people were careful to do what

he said. He and all the nobles helped the Jewish people strike down those who were trying to harm them. "The tables were turned and the Jews got the upper hand

over those who hated them" (9:1).

Through Esther, God delivered the Jewish people and gave them victory over their enemies. "Their sorrow was turned into joy and their mourning into a day of celebration" (9:22).

Purim is still celebrated today with the reading of

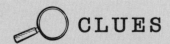

CLUES

The modern-day Feast of Lots, called Purim, was started to celebrate God's faithfulness to deliver the Jewish people. Because Esther stood up for what was right, the Jewish people were saved. This is similar to what Jesus has done for all of us. Just like the Jewish people were about to face death at the hands of Xerxes' original order, all of us deserve to die because of our sins. But because of what Jesus did on the cross, we have been given the offer of eternal life.

the book of Esther. It is called the Feast of Lots, because Haman cast lots to determine the day that the Jews would be destroyed (9:24).

The book of Esther notes that Mordecai

became the second-highest-ranking official behind the king. He was well respected because he "worked for the good of his people and spoke up for the welfare of all the Jews" (10:3).

Things changed for Esther and Mordecai. They went from being alone to being heroes in God's epic plan. They no longer lived in fear because of their culture. They had obeyed God and followed His commands. Things weren't always easy, but they didn't have time to complain. They both knew that God's ways are always the best!

Now that we've investigated Esther's story, it's time to think about some lessons we can learn from her life. All the way from orphan to queen, Esther did a lot of great kingdom work for the Lord.

Esther made sure that God was the most important thing in her life. She gathered the courage from Him to speak up for what was right—and in doing so, she saved her people.

God made your life very special too, and He has a wonderful story that He's using you to write. It's a story that will lead others to the good news of Jesus!

Let's look at each one of these valuable lessons individually along with some memory verses that will help plant God's truth in our hearts.

Power-Up #1:

GOD IS ALWAYS WITH US.

Esther was an orphan, but just because she surely felt alone without her mother and father, that didn't mean God had abandoned her. He *never* abandons His people. Esther had faith in the promises of her heavenly Father. This gave her the courage to stand up to her enemy and trust that God had her back.

God was with Esther and delivered her and her people from the wickedness of Haman's hatred. Esther knew that it was important to trust that God was always with her and not doubt His eternal goodness. When the time came for Esther to make big decisions, she did not shy away in fear. Be encouraged by the fact that you are very important to God, and know that He is using you to do great things.

MEMORY VERSE: "The LORD your God is with you, the Mighty Warrior who saves. He will take great delight in you." Zephaniah 3:17

Power-Up #2:
YOU MATTER.

You were created for a very special purpose. The God of the universe thought about you, and your life was made to glorify Him and reflect His goodness in a hurting world. It didn't matter what Esther's background was. It didn't matter that she was different than the people around her. She put her faith in the promises of God and gave the outcome of her life to Him. It's important to learn this lesson as you follow God. No matter what grade you're in, no matter how much money your family has or doesn't have, never forget that you matter to God.

Just like Esther found herself in the role of queen, she knew that she could never have gotten there without God's help.

That's the cool thing about Esther's story. She didn't wake up one day and wish to become married to the king of the greatest kingdom on earth. Esther simply made the most of every situation she was in and left the results to God. She didn't find her self-worth in material possessions or in the words of others. Esther put her trust in what God said about her! Living from that perspective helped Esther have the strength to stand up for what was right and save her people.

MEMORY VERSE: For you created my inmost being; you knit me together in my mother's womb. I praise you because I am fearfully and wonderfully made. Psalm 139:13–14

Power-Up #3:
GOD DELIVERS.

Esther knew that she couldn't convince the king without God's help. She had to act on truth but understood that any power she had as queen was given to her not by Xerxes but by God. Esther couldn't live each day in fear of the unknown but rather in faith that God would bring her to all the people and places that He wanted her to meet and see. She knew that God was with her everywhere she went.

God loves you and is with you through all the ups and downs of life. God isn't there just on the good days. Be confident, like Esther, that God is your Deliverer, all the time.

MEMORY VERSE: "Be strong and courageous. Do not be afraid or terrified because of them, for the Lord your God goes with you; he will never leave you nor forsake you."
Deuteronomy 31:6

Power-Up #4:
DON'T LET FEAR
KEEP YOU FROM GOD.

There were plenty of times in Esther's life when she could have let fear stop her. When Mordecai told her about Haman's terrible plan, Esther knew it would take courage to approach the king. Her one bold decision to move forward with God's guidance and ask the king for help saved so many people. When fear creeps in, putting faith in God is the key. Overcome the struggles by trusting in God, who loves you more than anything. Haman was a grown-up bully, and Esther could have let fear keep her from standing up to him. Thankfully, she put her trust in God.

Remember that fear doesn't always come from other people. Sometimes it might come from inside us—in our thoughts, for example. That's when we have to act like Esther and rely on God's truth. We constantly have to read our Bibles and get help from other believers as we learn how to overcome fear.

MEMORY VERSE: When I am afraid, I put my trust in you. Psalm 56:3

Power-Up #5:
BE HUMBLE.

Sometimes it's hard to do the right thing. Sometimes it's hard to be patient and love other people when they act unlovable. Esther is a good role model in humility. At every turn, we read that she was finding favor with all the people in her life. She respected the wishes of Mordecai when he told her not to mention her heritage, and she kept that humble spirit all the way through the process of becoming queen. Like Esther, we should make it our goal to act in gentleness and love no matter what situation we're in.

Finding your value in who God says you are really makes all the difference. Knowing that you are a child of the King helps keep your heart filled with His eternal love. Esther understood this. The Bible says that she was very pretty, but that wasn't where her courage came from. When Mordecai told Esther not to mention her background, she humbly obeyed. Even when she became queen, Esther still honored Mordecai's request. She waited until the right time before taking action. Esther didn't jump ahead of God's plan.

MEMORY VERSE: Be completely humble and gentle; be patient, bearing with one another in love. Ephesians 4:2

Power-Up #6:
STAND UP FOR WHAT'S RIGHT.

Sometimes it's easier to avoid making hard choices. Maybe you know someone at school who is getting picked on or doesn't have any friends. We can learn from Esther's life that standing up for what's right may not be easy, but it's necessary. God was always with Esther, just like He's always with us. When the time came for Esther to approach the king for help in protecting her people, she stood up for what was right and didn't back down. This part of Esther's story shows that even if a choice is hard to make, if it's the right one, then make it—knowing that God is the One giving you the strength you need to succeed.

Who knows what would have happened if Esther hadn't stood up for her people? Most likely, things would have been very bad. Haman, after all, was a very evil person. Like Esther, we need to always be ready to do the right thing that honors God and helps protect and care for others.

MEMORY VERSE: And whatever you do, whether in word or deed, do it all in the name of the Lord Jesus, giving thanks to God the Father through him. Colossians 3:17

Power-Up #7:
BE WISE.

Being wise will help us connect with God. Esther was wise because she kept herself living daily life in a humble way. She learned to listen and take instructions from others. She didn't become selfish and only want her way of doing things. She learned to submit her will to the Lord and simply obey God.

God kept opening all the right doors for Esther, and she eventually became queen. She connected with God as she lived her life making wise decisions. For example, a wise decision is to do your homework and do it well. But sometimes you may not want to do it. Being wise in this situation will help you stay committed to your schoolwork, and you will be a better student because of it. Esther also gained wisdom by listening. She listened to Mordecai and was willing to risk her own safety because she knew what was true. Esther was wise in how she interacted with the king. She respected his position but wasn't afraid to speak truth. She used wisdom to make smart decisions that ultimately saved many lives.

MEMORY VERSE: "Therefore everyone who hears these words of mine and puts them into practice is like a wise man who built his house on the rock." Matthew 7:24

Power-Up #8:

TREAT OTHERS WITH RESPECT.

Esther decided that being obedient to God was a smart choice. She understood how important it is to live unselfishly by thinking about other people. Esther knew that the way she treated other people mattered. Esther understood that other people were created by God too, and that she had to believe that the way she treated them was the way she was treating God.

When she was in the royal palace being taken care of and given special things, Esther still listened to Mordecai and respected his wishes not to mention her background.

Later, when Mordecai told her she needed to go to the king to save her people, Esther asked for prayer and said she would be fasting and praying too. Esther knew many things would compete for her attention and cause her to want to be selfish, but ultimately she had peace knowing that God was showing her how to serve others.

MEMORY VERSE: "Truly I tell you, whatever you did not do for one of the least of these, you did not do for me." Matthew 25:45

Power-Up #9:
BE COURAGEOUS.

Esther knew that God was in control of her life and the lives of her people. Still, she knew she had to act when it came time for her to help her people. Esther stepped out in courage even when she thought that approaching King Xerxes may have meant she'd lose her life. Being a part of God's kingdom work means being courageous in the face of hard times. God is the Creator. He made you to do things. He gave you a purpose. Rely on Him today, and go with courage to do great things for His glory. You are not alone. In God you are powerful and loved.

Sometimes things will happen that might make you feel insecure and weak. You might feel like you can't make a difference or help somebody. The truth is, with God's help, you can be a courageous person who cares for others, just like Esther cared. You can stand up and help someone know that they matter too. Throughout the Bible, God gives us the command to be strong and take courage. Take your courage from God as you wait on Him to direct your path.

MEMORY VERSE: For the Spirit God gave us does not make us timid, but gives us power, love and self-discipline. 2 Timothy 1:7

Power-Up #10:

GOD IS BIGGER THAN OUR PROBLEMS.

Just like Esther, we have problems. Everyone does. But Esther saw God as big and mighty, in control over everything, including her problems. Esther didn't let her problems overwhelm her. She kept her faith in God, knowing that the One who is all-powerful is bigger than the stressful times. Esther kept her eyes on God as she confronted the difficult times in her life.

What is it that you're worried about? What is that one problem in your life that seems to keep you down? Please don't forget that God is infinitely more powerful than anything. Have faith, like Esther, that God will never let you go or let you down.

Esther knew that God made her and loved her: not because Esther was queen, not because she was married to a powerful king, and not because of the size of the king's army. Esther knew that God alone could and would create a way through life's problems. She just had to stay connected to Him, and we need to do the same!

Esther found all of her hope in God. That way she wouldn't be let down. Picture God standing between you and the problems you are facing.

MEMORY VERSE: "Ah, Sovereign LORD, you have made the heavens and the earth by your great power and outstretched arm. Nothing is too hard for you." Jeremiah 32:17

Matt Koceich is a husband,
father, and public school teacher.
He and his family live in Texas.

Collect Them All!

Kingdom Files: Who Is Jesus?

This biblically accurate biography explores the life of Jesus while drawing readers into a fascinating time and place as they learn about the One who gave sight to the blind, made the lame to walk, raised people from the dead, and who died so that we might live.

Paperback / 978-1-68322-626-0 / $4.99

Kingdom Files: Who Was Daniel?

This biblically accurate biography explores the life of Daniel while drawing readers into a fascinating time and place as they learn about the faithful man of God who interpreted dreams for the king and ultimately survived a den of hungry lions.

Paperback / 978-1-68322-627-7 / $4.99

Kingdom Files: Who Was David?

This biblically accurate biography explores the life of David while drawing readers into a fascinating time and place as they learn about the shepherd boy turned king who played a harp and slayed a giant with a stone and a sling.

Paperback / 978-1-68322-628-4 / $4.99

Kingdom Files: Who Was Jonah?

This biblically accurate biography explores the life of Jonah while drawing readers into a fascinating time and place as they learn about the reluctant prophet who said "no" to God, was tossed overboard during a storm, and swallowed by a giant fish.

Paperback / 978-1-68322-630-7 / $4.99

Kingdom Files: Who Was Mary, Mother of Jesus?

This biblically accurate biography explores the life of Mary while drawing readers into a fascinating time and place as they learn about the courageous young teenager who said "yes" to God and ultimately gave birth to the Savior of the world.

Paperback / 978-1-68322-631-4 / $4.99

Excited for More?

Here's a sneak peek of
Kingdom Files: Who Was David?

Early Life

To begin our investigation into the life of David, it helps to understand a few background notes first. David's story is found in the Old Testament books of 1 Samuel, 2 Samuel, 1 Kings, and 1 Chronicles. When David was young, a king named Saul had ruled over the land of Israel for forty-two years. He became selfish, so God decided to call a new young man to take the throne.

God sent his prophet, Samuel, to David's house. So Samuel went to Bethlehem where he found a man named Jesse, who was David's father. David was the youngest of eight sons. He worked as a shepherd tending his father's

flock. Jesse introduced his sons to Samuel, but the prophet asked if there were any others. That's when Jesse called for David, and immediately Samuel knew this was who he was supposed to anoint as king. The Bible says that at this point, the Spirit of God came on David with power (1 Samuel 16:13).

Meanwhile, King Saul was being attacked
by an evil spirit. He asked his servants to bring
someone who could play music to help calm his

nerves. The
servants knew
about David,
and so Jesse
sent his son
David to Saul
with a donkey
loaded with
bread and wine
and a young
goat as gifts for the king. Saul was so pleased with
David and his music playing that he had David
stay with him to be in his service.

At the same time, there was an army called
the Philistines who were close by, trying to

attack the Israelites. King Saul gathered the
Israelites to fight
and defend their
towns (1 Samuel
17:2–3). When
they went out to
engage in battle,
Saul and his men
were confronted
by a horrifying
sight. There was
one Philistine
in particular
named Goliath.

The Bible says that
Goliath was over
nine feet tall and
wore a bronze hel-
met and armor that

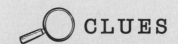

CLUES

Even the giant's spear had
a fifteen-pound iron point!

weighed 125 pounds!

The giant began taunting the king and his army. Goliath yelled out a challenge. He asked for a man who would be willing to fight him. He said that if he won, the Israelites would become slaves to the Philistines; and if one of Saul's men won, the Philistines would become servants to the Israelites. King Saul was terrified! (1 Samuel 17:11).

This exchange went on for forty days. Morning and night, Goliath approached the Israelites, asking for a man who would be willing to fight. No one dared fight the superhuman giant.

Meanwhile, David was in charge of taking food to his older brothers. They were a part of the Israelite army and within clear view of the giant. David ran out to the battle lines to check on his brothers and make sure they were okay. As soon as David saw Goliath, he wanted to know who

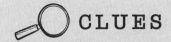

CLUES

David told Saul about how when lions or bears would come to capture the sheep, he would go after the predators and save the sheep from being eaten. He also added that if the animal tried to attack him, he was strong enough to take its life. David then compared Goliath to the wild animals: "The LORD who rescued me from the paw of the lion and the paw of the bear will rescue me from the hand of this Philistine" (1 Samuel 17:37).

he was. David was upset because of the way the giant didn't respect God (1 Samuel 17:26).

David's oldest brother was angry at him, because he thought David was only there to watch a good fight. Saul heard about David's courage and sent for him. In the king's chambers, David told Saul not to lose heart because of Goliath's threats. And then David offered to go and fight the giant!

Saul wasn't convinced. He thought David was too young and unable to win a battle with the giant. Saul added that Goliath had been a warrior for a very long time. But David was ready with a reply. He told Saul about his job tending sheep.

King Saul finally agreed to let David go and fight the giant. He began by putting his personal armor on David. But David couldn't move around in the heavy armor. David armed himself with only his staff and his sling, and he chose five stones from a nearby stream and put them in a pouch. Then he went out to meet Goliath.

The superhuman laughed. "Am I a dog, that you come at me with sticks? . . . Come here. . . and I'll give your flesh to the birds and the wild animals!" (1 Samuel 17:43–44). David knew that God was on his side and responded to the giant not with fear but with courage. "You come against me with sword and spear and javelin, but I come against you in the name of the LORD Almighty"

(1 Samuel 17:45). David said that he was confident that God would deliver the giant into his hands. And then he added that after he won the battle, the

whole world would know that God was in charge.

David also said that the battle belonged to God and that God would give not only Goliath, but all the Philistines, into the Israelites' hands. At that, the giant moved quickly to attack David. David didn't hesitate. He ran toward the giant. As he ran, David took a stone and slung it at Goliath. The stone hit the giant on the forehead, causing him to fall dead "facedown on the ground" (1 Samuel 17:49). At the sight of this unbelievable event, the Philistines took off running. David kept Goliath's weapons. King Saul was very impressed that David had taken care of the wicked giant and a very massive problem!